HISPANIC AMERICA

1950s TO 1960s

BY
RICHARD WORTH

Marshall Cavendish
Benchmark
New York

Thanks to Stephen Pitti, professor of history and American studies at Yale University, for his expert reading of this manuscript.

MARSHALL CAVENDISH BENCHMARK
99 WHITE PLAINS ROAD
TARRYTOWN, NEW YORK 10591-5502
www.marshallcavendish.us

Text copyright © 2010 by Marshall Cavendish Corporation

LIBRARY OF CONGRESS CATALOGING-IN-PUBLICATION DATA
Worth, Richard.
1950s to 1960s / by Richard Worth.
p. cm. — (Hispanic America)
Includes bibliographical references and index.
Summary: "Provides comprehensive information on the history of the Spanish coming to the United States, focusing on the decades of the 1950s and 1960s"—Provided by publisher.
ISBN 978-0-7614-4177-9
1. Hispanic Americans—History—20th century—Juvenile literature. 2. Hispanic Americans—Social condtions—20th century—Juvenile literature. 3. Immigrants—United States—History—20th century—Juvenile literature. 4. United States—Race relations—History—20th century—Juvenile literature. 5. United States—Emigration and immigration—History—20th century—Juvenile literature. 6. Latin America—Emigration and immigration—History—20th century—Juvenile literature. I. Title. II. Title: Nineteen fifties to nineteen sixties.
E184.S75W675 2009
305.868'073—dc22
2008028195

Poem on page 63 is from *I am Joaquin/Yo soy Joaquín* (Bantam, 1972).

Photo research by Tracey Engel

Cover: *Corbis*: Hulton-Deutsch Collection
Title page: Custom Medical Stock Photo / M. English, MD
Back cover: Prints & Photographs Division, LC-DIG-nclc-04522
The photographs in this book are used by permission and through the courtesy of:
AP/Wide World Photos: 31, 35, 58-59, 68-69, 71. *Cesar Chavez Foundation*: 25, 27. *Corbis*: Russell Lee, 8, 10; Bettmann, 14-15, 17, 19, 50, 53, 56, 62, 67; Ted Streshinsky, 1, 22, 33. *Getty Images*: Harry Pennington/Keystone Features, 20; Michael Rougier//Time Life Pictures, 28, 40-41; Keystone, 44; Alan Band/Fox Photos, 47; Roy Stevens/Time & Life Pictures, 48. *The Granger Collection, New York*: 4. *Library of Congress, Prints & Photographs Division*: LC-DIG-nclc-04522, 36; LC-DIG-ppmsc-03256, 39. *North Wind Picture Archives*: 7. *The Roybal family*: 13

EDITOR: Joy Bean   PUBLISHER: Michelle Bisson
ART DIRECTOR: Anahid Hamparian   SERIES DESIGNER: Kristen Branch

Printed in Malaysia
1 3 5 6 4 2

CONTENTS

CHAPTER ONE

DEALING WITH DISCRIMINATION

AS THE DECADE OF THE 1950S BEGAN, Edward R. Roybal took his seat as a newly elected member of the Los Angeles City Council in California. He was the only Mexican American who served on the council, which was run by white Anglos who governed the city of Los Angeles.

Roybal was born in 1916 in New Mexico and his ancestors had first settled around Albuquerque in the 1600s. Spanish settlers began making their mark when, in 1492, they began coming to the United States in search of riches and with the hope of spreading their religious beliefs. Over the years they had created an enormous empire in the Americas, contolling most of South America, Central America, Caribbean islands, and the American West, where Roybal's family had lived for many generations.

Opposite:
The Spanish first began to arrive in the New World in the late 1400s, looking to conquer lands and spread their religious beliefs. Here, Vasco Nuñez de Balboa takes possession of the Pacific Ocean for Spain in September of 1513.

When Roybal was six, his parents moved to Los Angeles, California. He grew up in the Boyle Heights *barrio* of the city. By the 1930s, Los Angeles had a population of almost one million Mexicans, the largest number outside of Mexico City. But Hispanics faced severe discrimination in politics, employment, and education. Nevertheless, this situation would begin to change with Roybal's election in 1949 and other developments during the 1950s and 1960s.

HERITAGE FROM THE PAST

The story of Mexican Americans begins with the Mexican War, which took place from 1846–1848. The war started when an American army invaded Mexico and defeated the Mexican army. The United States took control of California and the Southwest, and thousands of Mexicans who lived there suddenly became U.S. citizens. The Treaty of Guadalupe Hidalgo, signed by the United States and Mexico at the end of the war, was supposed to protect Mexican Americans' land. In many cases, the land had been held by Mexican American families for generations, but the treaty did not safeguard their property. In California, for example, the Mexican land grants were challenged by Anglos, and their claims were supported by American courts. Mexican American families hired lawyers to defend their land rights, but the legal fees were very high, and, in the end, many people were forced to sell their lands to the Anglos for small amounts of money. As a result, the Mexican Americans

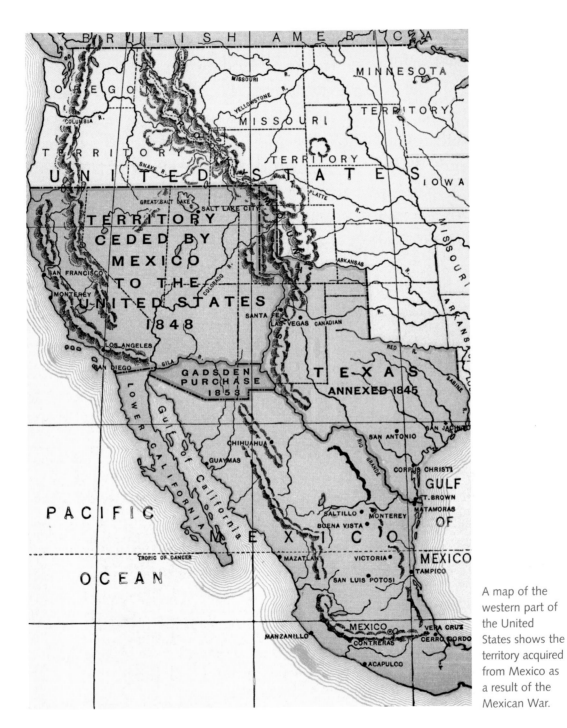

A map of the western part of the United States shows the territory acquired from Mexico as a result of the Mexican War.

ended up working on their own estates, but were now employed by the new Anglo land owners.

In the Southwest, Mexican Americans found themselves reduced to the status of second-class citizens. Anglo cattle ranchers tried to drive Mexican sheep owners off their lands. As large farms, mines, and railroads were developed, Mexicans were forced to fill low-paying, unskilled jobs. "For example, in ranching," wrote historians Luis M. Falcón and Dan Gilbarg in *Handbook of Hispanic Cultures in the United States: Sociology*, "Mexicans were the cowhands,

A number of Mexicans in the United States found the only work they could get was manual labor, such as working on railroads or picking crops.

but only Anglos were the overseers. . . . In the railroads, Mexicans worked in construction and the maintenance of the tracks, while only Anglos worked as engineers, motormen, and conductors. On the farms, Mexicans picked the crops, but only Anglos served as counters and packers in the sheds." In short, Anglos had all the higher paying, skilled jobs, while Mexican Americans were prevented from filling them.

During the early part of the twentieth century, a violent revolution broke out in Mexico.

It was aimed at overthrowing a brutal dictatorship. By 1930, approximately 1.5 million Mexicans had escaped the violence and crossed the 2,000-mile (3,218-kilometer) border between Mexico and the United States. Some of them were given *visas* by the U.S. government, permitting them to become residents. But many others entered the United States illegally. Nevertheless, Mexicans were generally welcomed by Anglo farm owners who desperately needed them to work in the fields. Mexican families picked cotton in Texas and harvested fruits and vegetables in California. They worked for very low wages, enabling farm owners to reap larger profits from the sale of their crops. Those Mexican Americans who worked in manufacturing and small businesses were usually restricted to unskilled jobs and paid less than Anglos.

Meanwhile, very few Mexican Americans had an opportunity to improve their position in society because they lacked a good education. In Texas, for example, many Mexican American children were forced to attend segregated schools or segregated classrooms in Anglo schools—where they were separated from Anglo children. One reason, wrote historian William Vélez in *Handbook of Hispanic Cultures in the United States: Sociology*, was "the perception among Anglo parents that Mexicans had lower standards of cleanliness and were socially and economically inferior."

The segregated schools were far inferior to the schools for white children. The teachers were often untrained.

The children of Mexicans were sometimes forced to leave school and work in the fields in order to help earn money for the family.

There were no blackboards in the classrooms, and the children had no desks or chairs, in contrast to the schools for white children. Many children did not attend school because they worked in the fields with their parents. Adults received such low wages that they were forced to depend on the money that their children earned. According to one study, there was an attitude among Texans that if Mexican children went to school, they would not be available to work on the white-owned farms.

During the 1940s and 1950s, the Mexican schoolchildren often faced serious problems. Their teachers were frequently

Anglos who drilled them in English and encouraged them to forget Spanish, their native language. As a result, according to Professor George I. Sanchez in *A Documentary History of Mexican Americans*, a child "cannot speak to the teacher and is unable to understand what goes on . . . in the classroom." Although children learned English, school did not seem to relate to their lives. "Most of these children leave school before they have learned enough to help them become effective in improving their environmental conditions," Sanchez wrote.

Most Mexican American children were also given courses in vocational education, such as farmwork, auto repair, and metal repair. This prepared them to hold low-paying, unskilled jobs.

CHALLENGING THE SCHOOL SYSTEM IN THE 1950s

Beginning in the 1940s, Mexican-American organizations began to challenge inequality in public schools. The League of United Latin American Citizens (LULAC) assisted Mexican American parents in Los Angeles in fighting segregation. In the late 1940s, LULAC attorneys won the case *Mendez v. Westminster School District*, whose outcome outlawed segregated schools in the Los Angeles area. At about the same time, LULAC won a similar case in Texas. Nevertheless, California and Texas acted slowly to eliminate their segregated schools.

LULAC continued its campaign to end school segregation during the 1950s. Another Mexican American group called the American G.I. Forum joined them in this effort. The forum had been founded in Corpus Christi, Texas, in 1948 by Dr. Hector P. Garcia, a World War II veteran. Thousands of Mexican Americans had fought in World War II. Thirteen had been awarded the Congressional Medal of Honor—America's highest award for bravery in battle. The forum pressured the U.S. government into providing Mexican American war veterans with all the benefits due to soldiers under the G.I. Bill of Rights. The G.I. Bill was supposed to pay for higher education, but this benefit had been denied to Mexican American veterans.

LITTLE SCHOOLS

During the 1950s, LULAC established an educational project called Little Schools of the 400. These schools enrolled Mexican American preschool children. Teachers in the schools taught these children, who spoke only Spanish, four hundred English words that they would use most often in school. This education would help them succeed in first grade. Beginning with only sixty students, the schools were soon teaching more than four hundred pupils each month.

THE STRUGGLE FOR EQUALITY

It was against a background of discrimination that Edward Roybal grew up in Los Angeles. Roybal recalled that when he was dating a young woman during the 1940s, he was approached by a white police officer. Roybal and the young woman, who later became his wife, were "sharing chili beans and crackers at a stand at Fourth and Soto streets in Boyle Heights," wrote George Ramos, a reporter for the *Los Angeles Times*, in an article. The policeman "went through Roybal's pockets. The officer then dumped the couple's dinner on the sidewalk."

After serving in World War II like thousands of other Mexican Americans, Roybal returned to California. There he became director of health education for the Los Angeles County Tuberculosis Health Association. In 1947, he ran for the Los Angeles City Council in the Ninth District. This district included Boyle Heights, where he had grown up and where half the population were Hispanic or African American. Nevertheless, he was defeated by a white politician named Parley P. Christensen. Many Hispanics did not vote in the election or

Edward Roybal was a Mexican American who ran for city council in Los Angeles.

participate in politics. They knew that the city council was controlled by Anglos who had very little interest in fighting for their needs. Some Mexican Americans were also illegal immigrants who were afraid that if they tried to vote, they might be sent back to Mexico by the police.

Following his defeat, Roybal, age thirty-one, started the Community Service Organization (CSO) with the help of a local organizer named Fred Ross. Ross believed that organizing was a way of "providing people with the opportunity to become aware of their own capabilities and potential." The mission of the CSO was to register Mexican Americans so they could vote in local elections and change the government of the city of Los Angeles. The CSO would become one of the primary organizations that changed living and working conditions for *Hispanic Americans* during the 1950s and 1960s. "The war was the catalyst," Roybal recalled in *La Raza*, by author Stan Steiner. "Thousands of Hispanic Americans had fought during World War II and many had died. Those who returned faced the same discrimination that they had left behind. They decided to do something about it."

Opposite: Fred Ross (in glasses on left) ran Edward Roybal's campaign for city councilman in 1949. He also worked to support the United Farm Workers's cause.

The CSO registered 15,000 new voters in the Hispanic areas of the Ninth District. It also reached out to gather support among labor unions, the Catholic Church in Los Angeles, and the Jewish community in the city. Early in 1949, Roybal left his position as head of the CSO to run for city councilman from the Ninth

DEALING WITH DISCRIMINATION
15

District. Running his campaign were Fred Ross as well as members of the Latino community. As Roybal went door-to-door asking residents to vote for him, his home served as a center for campaign workers. They sent out appeals for support through the mail. On election day, Roybal defeated Parley Christensen and won the council seat—the first Mexican American to win this position.

As Kenneth Burt wrote in *Public Affairs Report*, "He had gone from a candidate to a cause. He was now the very personification of Mexican Americans on the move, a symbol of Latino [Hispanic] aspirations. He stood for a community engaged in civic life and desirous of the American dream: a solid job, home ownership, health care, and an education for the children."

BRACERO PROGRAM AND OPERATION WETBACK

Roybal served on the city council for fifteen years. During that period he battled to end discrimination in education, housing, and employment. In 1962, he was elected to the U.S. Congress, the first Hispanic to hold a congressional seat in California since the 1870s. During the 1940s and 1950s, Roybal and other Hispanic political leaders dealt with several difficult issues. In the 1940s, the United States had signed an agreement with Mexico called the *Bracero program. Bracero* is a Spanish word that means "one who works with his arms, or *brazos.*" This program was designed to bring Mexican laborers into the United States to replace

Americans who were fighting in World War II. The program was so successful that it continued into the 1950s and early 1960s. During the years that the Bracero program operated, as many as five million Mexicans may have crossed the border to work in the United States.

Most of the braceros, as they were called, worked in the grape vineyards, fruit orchards, and vegetable fields in California and the Southwest. Gathering at Mexican border towns, the braceros were taken into the United States. There they were hired by farmers at employment centers in El Paso, Texas, and other U.S. cities. Braceros were supposed to be provided with adequate housing, given good food, and paid at the same rate as Anglo workers in the

These braceros, part of the Bracero program, eat lunch in the fields in which they work.

United States. But farmers often violated these rules. Nevertheless, braceros continued crossing the border because the rate of pay was higher than what they received in Mexico. Meanwhile, American farmers obtained cheap labor to plant and harvest their crops.

In addition to the braceros, an increasing number of Mexicans were crossing the border illegally. There were not enough jobs in Mexico for everyone who wanted to work. So Mexicans looked to *El Norte*—the North and the United States. Many of these illegal immigrants were assisted by people called *coyotes*. These are people who help immigrants cross the border illegally. Sometimes the illegal immigrants swam across the Rio Grande River, which runs along part of the border between Mexico and the United States. As a result, the immigrants were often called the offensive term *wetbacks*. Sometimes the coyotes hid Mexican immigrants in trucks or in the trunks of cars and brought them through checkpoints on the border. There were too few U.S. border guards to search every car that passed through a checkpoint or patrol the 2,000-mile (3,219-km) border with Mexico. Not enough guards meant more people could sneak through.

During the 1950s, concern about the illegal immigrants grew. The cold war, the political conflict between the United States and what was then the Soviet Union, was intense. American officials began investigating suspected Soviet agents who they thought might have infiltrated

In order to find jobs and make a better life for themselves, some Mexicans came into the United States illegally by crossing the Rio Grande River in Texas.

the U.S. government and other organizations. All foreign-born people living in the United States suddenly became suspect. Congress also introduced the Subversive Registration Bill. This required Americans to sign oaths stating their loyalty to the United States. Many people believed that being forced to sign such an oath called into question their loyalty as United States citizens. Roybal strongly opposed the bill. His vote was very courageous because it could have cost him reelection. Nevertheless, he held his seat on the council in the next election and served until 1962.

Fear of immigrants also led the Republican administration of President Dwight Eisenhower to begin Operation Wetback in June 1954. Under Operation Wetback, the U.S. Border Patrol rounded up more than one million immigrants—both legal and illegal—and shipped them back to Mexico. Some families were broken apart, as members

Members of the Texas Border Patrol guard illegal Mexican immigrants in 1948. They were captured close to the Mexican border.

who had come to the United States illegally were forced to leave their homes. Many Anglos supported the program. Although Mexican Americans had been eagerly accepted and employed by farmers who needed field workers, they were not protected by the laws of the United States.

During the next decade, however, this situation would begin to change.

CHAPTER TWO

A Rising Tide

DURING THE EARLY 1950S, THE COMMUNITY Service Organization led by Fred Ross established chapters across the state of California. In 1953, Ross came to San Jose, looking for someone to help him set up a new chapter in that city. Ross had already received the names of several people, one of whom was already trying to organize poor Mexican American agricultural workers. His name was César Chávez.

Born in 1927, Chávez had spent the early years of his life in Arizona where his parents—Librado and Juana—owned a farm and a general store. But in 1929, a severe economic downturn known as the Great Depression began. The Depression cost millions of Americans their jobs and their businesses. Among them were Librado and Juana Chávez, who lost their farm and

Opposite: César Chávez became an important role model in the fight for workers' rights.

were forced to move to California, where they became migrant farm workers.

For more than a decade, the Chávez family moved from one big farm to another, harvesting lettuce or cotton, sugar beets, or melons. It was grueling, low-paid labor with children working side by side with their parents in the fields. Like so many other migrants, the Chávez family earned barely enough to feed themselves and put gas in their old car to drive on to the next harvest. "In Oxnard, [California,] the Chávez family had to spend one winter living in a tent that was soggy from rain and fog," wrote biographers Richard Griswold Del Castillo and Richard A. Garcia in *César Chávez, A Triumph of Spirit.* "They used a 50-gallon can for a stove and tried to keep wood for fuel dry inside the tent. The children did odd jobs around town; the adults tried to find work."

When Chávez was not working, he attended school. But there he encountered cruel discrimination, according to Del Castillo and Garcia. "When you went into school for the first time," Chávez recalled, "the principal and a teacher would discuss where they should put you, right in front of you. They would make you run laps around the track if they caught you speaking Spanish, or a teacher in a classroom would make you write 'I won't speak Spanish' on the board three hundred times, or I remember once a teacher hung a sign on me that said 'I am a clown, I speak Spanish.'" Restaurants had signs in the windows that said

White Trade Only, and Mexican Americans were forced to sit in segregated sections of movie theaters.

During the 1940s, Chávez joined the navy and served in World War II on Guam, an island in the Pacific Ocean. Three years after his return, he married Helen Fabela. The couple lived in Delano, California, where Chávez worked in the fields. Eventually, the couple moved to San Jose, after Chávez found a job in a lumber business. Helen and César, along with their growing family, which eventually included eight children, lived in a small house in the Mexican American barrio.

César Chávez while in the navy.

In 1952, Chávez had begun helping a local Catholic priest, Father Donald McDonnell, provide church services to migrant workers in the fields around San Jose. Since early childhood, when he had been taught Catholicism by his grandmother, Chávez had been deeply religious. From his experiences as a migrant worker, he also realized that the poorly paid field hands needed something in addition to religion. They had to organize if they ever hoped to improve their lives.

Father McDonnell had passed along Chávez's name to Fred Ross when he heard that the CSO was looking for an organizer in San Jose. At first, Chávez was not interested in meeting Ross. He believed Ross was a uniformed Anglo who knew very little about the problems of Hispanic field workers. In June 1952, however, Chávez finally agreed to talk with Ross, and what he heard impressed him.

Ross explained what the CSO had done to sign up Mexican American voters, the victory of Ed Roybal in Los Angeles, and the efforts by the organization to fight police brutality against Hispanics. Indeed, a year earlier, after Anglo policemen had almost killed some Mexican American young people, the CSO had pressured the Los Angeles police department into firing them. In their book *The Fight in the Fields: César Chávez and the Farmworkers Movement*, Susan Ferriss and Ricardo Sandoval described the meeting between Ross and Chávez. "Never before in the whole history of Los Angeles had any cop ever gotten 'canned' [fired] for beating up a Mexican American," Ross said. "If the people of Los Angeles could do it . . . there was no reason why we couldn't do the same sort of thing . . . if we wanted to badly enough."

CSO AND A UNION

Chávez was convinced that the CSO was an organization where he could make a difference. He decided to join it and work with Ross. Nervous at first, Chávez gradually developed confidence as he went door-to-door among Mexican American families, trying to sign them up as new voters. Although many of them had lived in the United States for

years, they had never filled out the papers to become citizens. Mexican Americans also mistrusted the Anglo-controlled local government, which had done little for them living in the barrios.

While he was signing up voters, Chávez was also working with Mexican American field hands. Under the Bracero Program, big growers received permission from the California state government to sign up braceros if there was a shortage of migrant workers. Since the braceros worked for lower wages than the local workers, the growers often

César Chávez (on right) and other CSO members during a voter registration drive in the 1950s.

LIFE IN THE BARRIOS

The San Jose barrio where César Chávez and his family lived was a rundown section of the city with no paved streets. It was much like other barrios where Mexican Americans lived. The resident of another barrio located in McAllen, Texas, described it this way to author Stan Steiner: "We have to buy water in jugs, or bring it home in barrels. No water! No sanitation! No drainage in the streets! No sewers! . . . My neighbor has no electric lights, right in the middle of the city. Across the street, in that house you see, half of the floors are earth. The good earth! Housing in these barrios is ten times worse than the worst slum in any northern city."

claimed there was a shortage, even when one did not exist, just to save money. Under pressure from powerful growers, the local officials brought in braceros and refused to hire the farmhands who lived around Oxnard, California. Working with the CSO, Chávez exposed this situation and eventually forced state officials to hire local workers.

By this time Chávez had become a full-time employee of the CSO. His organizing work was so successful that in 1959 he became executive director of the organization. At the same time, the political strength of Hispanic voters was beginning to grow. In 1960, a group of Mexican American political leaders met in Fresno, California, where they formed the Mexican American Political Association (MAPA). The first president was Edward Roybal. The MAPA was aimed at organizing Mexican American voters so they could help elect officials who supported Hispanic rights. The MAPA helped establish Viva Kennedy Clubs in states such as Texas and California. They hoped to gather support in the Hispanic community for the election of Democratic candidate John F. Kennedy as president of the United States in 1960. They believed that Kennedy supported the rights of Hispanic Americans. In a close vote, Kennedy beat the Republican nominee, Richard Nixon.

But Chávez was convinced that voter registration drives were not enough to improve conditions of migrant workers in the fields. He wanted the CSO to establish a union, which would give the migrant workers more power in deal-

BERT CORONA

Among the men who helped establish the MAPA was Bert Corona.
He served as president of the organization in California during the
1960s. Born in El Paso, Texas, in 1918, Corona became a labor organizer in California during the late 1930s. Later he worked for the CSO
and became a friend of César Chávez. Meanwhile, Corona also served
as an important member of the National Mexican Brotherhood. This
group had chapters across the United States with a membership of
about 30,000 people. They helped organize unions to give Mexican
Americans more power in the workplace. Corona later became executive director of the organization—a position he held until his death in
2001. During his years as an activist, Corona learned how to deal with
the power of the Anglo establishment. It took time, patience, and an
effective strategy. According to author Stan Steiner, Corona explained
that he realized that, "Many of our political leaders do not want to
make their activities too well known to the Anglo. In these towns the
Anglo leadership is often very conservative. They are in control. . . . We
are quietly organizing. We have not taken on the power structure yet."

ing with the farm owners. At a meeting of the organization in 1962, he brought up this idea to the members. When they voted it down, Chávez decided that the time had come to leave his position at the CSO and strike out on his own.

CREATING THE NFWA

Chávez, along with his wife, Helen, and their family, moved to Delano in the Imperial Valley, California's agricultural heartland. Since the family had very little money, Helen went to work in the fields while her husband started to build his organization. The National Farm Workers Association (NFWA) was based on the Mexican American *mutualistas* that had arisen during the nineteenth century. These were associations that held social gatherings and helped new immigrants with small loans to tide them over while they found work. Running the NFWA out of his house, Chávez began to build a reputation for himself. Migrants recognized that he would help them and their families when growers refused to pay them or hospitals refused to serve them because they were poor Mexican Americans.

César Chávez fought to improve conditions of migrant workers and their children.

Meanwhile, Chávez traveled the valley trying to gather members for the NFWA. In this effort, he had the assistance of Dolores Huerta, another member of the CSO. Huerta had experience working at the California state capital in Sacramento, publicizing the CSO's programs among influential politicians. While she continued working for the organization, Huerta had helped Chávez found the NFWA and joined him in the organizing effort. Eventually, Huerta left the CSO to work full-time for the NFWA.

Building the organization proved to be a difficult job. Past efforts at organizing a union in the 1940s and 1950s had not been very successful. Migrants moved regularly, and many were illegal immigrants.

Chávez, Huerta, and the other leaders of the NFWA hoped to change this attitude, but the organizing effort was very slow. They had to live on financial assistance from friends and food from local workers while trying to convince Mexican American laborers to join their organization. While the NFWA was gathering strength, a group of Filipino grape pickers—immigrants from the Philippines who also worked in the California fields—decided to go on strike on September 16, 1965, Mexico's national independence day. They were protesting low wages and asked the NFWA to join them to give the strike greater power. At first, Chávez hesitated because the NFWA contained only 1,200 members. He feared that if the strike failed, it could mean the end of his organization.

Nevertheless, Chávez called a meeting of the membership at Delano's Our Lady of Guadalupe Church—named after the patron saint of Mexico. At a tumultuous meeting, the members voted for the *huelga*—the strike. Members of the NFWA walked off their jobs in the grape vineyards and began to form a picket line around the fields. They carried signs and the NFWA flag—a black eagle on a red circle—hoping to keep other workers from crossing the lines and harvesting the grapes.

Grape pickers carry American flags and National Farm Workers Association banners as they march along the road to protest their low wages and poor working conditions.

The growers fought back. Del Castillo and Garcia wrote that growers hired men "recruited from the cities to intimidate the strikers. They drove tractors between the pickets and the fields to choke the union people with dust. They sprayed them with chemicals and tried to intimidate them with shotguns and dogs. Sometimes they injured strikers. But when someone got hurt on the picket line, it often had the effect of provoking a sympathy walk-out by their [the growers'] own workers. The police almost never intervened to protect the picketers."

The strike occurred during a period of other protests across the United States. Civil rights demonstrators led by Reverend Dr. Martin Luther King Jr. were demanding equal rights for African Americans. The strike at Delano, called the Great Delano Grape Strike, caught the attention of the media. Volunteers from civil rights groups, churches, and college campuses joined the picket lines. Chávez called for a national boycott in supermarkets against the purchase of grapes. Then, in March 1966, Chávez led a 300-mile (402-km) march from Delano to Sacramento to appeal to California governor Edmund G. "Pat" Brown to intervene and recognize the rights of the farmworkers.

By this time, the publicity had become too much for one of the largest grape growers, Schenley Corporation. The company agreed to recognize the National Farm Workers Union. Schenley let it represent the interests of the workers, negotiating for an agreement to achieve higher pay and var-

César Chávez (center) takes part in a U.S. Senate Labor Subcommittee hearing during the Great Delano Grape Strike. He told the committee the strike would continue until the growers agreed to the demands of the workers.

ious benefits. As Castillo and Garcia wrote, "For the first time in U.S. history, a grassroots, farm-labor union had gained recognition by a corporation." Over the next two years, other growers followed, signing contracts with the union.

It was a defining moment in the history of the struggle by Hispanic Americans for equal rights. Indeed, after 1966, Mexican Americans in Texas, Illinois, and other states who had been inspired by the NFWA, began leading their own marches and civil rights campaigns.

CHAPTER THREE

Cuban Americans Struggling to Succeed

WHILE THE POWER OF MEXICAN AMERICANS was increasing, changes were also occurring within the Hispanic community in other parts of the United States. Among these was the Cuban American community. During the early twentieth century, a small number of Cuban immigrants worked in the cigar-making factories in Florida. A few had left the island to make names for themselves as professional baseball players in the United States. During the 1950s, Miami had also become a popular resort area for Cubans. The airplane fare from Havana to Miami was low, and each year as many as 50,000 Cuban tourists came to Florida.

By the middle of the twentieth century, there were also an estimated 124,000 Cubans living permanently in the United

Opposite: Cuban Americans, both children and adults, work in a cigar-making factory in Florida.

States. They lived in cities such as New York, New Orleans, and Tampa, Florida. In 1955, a young Cuban revolutionary named Fidel Castro visited a Cuban community of about 3,000 immigrants in Union City, New Jersey. Hoping to raise money to overthrow the dictatorship of Cuban president Fulgencio Batista, he spoke at a bar called *El Molino Rojo* (The Red Mill). His tour also took him to New York City. There he told a crowd of eight hundred people that many people were leaving Cuba to escape the brutal Batista regime.

Castro returned to Cuba, where he continued his efforts to remove the Batista government. By 1959, Castro had brought his *guerrillas* out of the hills of Cuba and successfully driven Batista off the island. Cubans who had escaped from the island to the United States were overjoyed to hear the news. "I was overwhelmed with emotion to hear that, at long last, the tyrant had been deposed," recalled José Martínez, a resident of Miami, in Alex Antón and Roger Hernández's *Cubans in America*.

Immediately after the overthrow of Batista, several thousand government officials left the island. They moved to Florida, only 90 miles (145 km) away, where a Cuban American community already existed. Meanwhile, Castro promised the Cuban people a democracy that would provide benefits to the peasants who had lived in poverty for generations. But it soon became clear that the Castro government had other plans. Fidel Castro was a Communist who believed in the economic programs of the Soviet Union. There the entire economy was run by the government. Castro planned on having his government take control of lands owned by well-to-do Cubans, instead of giving them to the Cuban peasants. Castro also began putting his government in charge of Cuba's businesses.

By mid-1959, large landowners were already leaving Cuba, and soon afterward merchants, teachers, and doctors also

Fidel Castro took control of Cuba in 1959, and Cubans soon after began to flee the country.

began emigrating from the island. They had been successful professionals in Cuba. But they decided to flee the island, believing that there was no freedom for them under the Castro regime. Most of them traveled only a short distance away to southern Florida and established themselves in the city of Miami. "We did not come as immigrants pulled by the American economic dream," said Cuban Nestor Carbonell in *Cubans in America*, "but as refugees pushed by the Cuban political nightmare."

The United States welcomed these immigrants, hoping to undermine Castro's government. Castro was already clamping a Communist dictatorship on the island and allying himself with the Soviet Union. In 1961, the U.S. government established the Cuban Refugee Program. This program provided financial assistance to Cuban immigrants for food, clothing, job training, health care, and even money for higher education. As Richard Brown, director of the Office of Refugee and Migration Affairs, put it, "Our assistance demonstrates in concrete form to the enslaved millions in Communist-dominated lands the inherent humanity of a free society."

In addition, the U.S. government established the Cuban Children's Program. This was called Operation Peter Pan, taking about 14,000 children

Opposite: The United States set up programs for children of those who fled Cuba. Here, a nursery school for Cuban refugees.

out of Cuba. They traveled without their parents to escape from Communism, which was being taught in Cuban schools. When they came to the United States, they lived in foster homes with American parents. American churches had done much of the work finding foster parents for the Cuban children to help them feel at home in the United States.

Nevertheless, Cubans often faced discrimination as they entered the United States. Some Anglos in Florida expressed anger and prejudice because so many Hispanic immigrants were coming to their cities. But the Cubans possessed something that Mexican Americans lacked—a much stronger self-image. As sociologist Lisandro Pérez has written in *Latinos*, "There is an absence of minority-group orientation. Cubans have a very high self-concept—at times there is a certain arrogance—that's very different from the self-concept of Mexican Americans and Puerto Ricans."

This self-image helped the Cubans deal more effectively with discrimination from the Anglos around Miami. The new immigrants established businesses in South Florida and loaned money to others to help them succeed. "The system worked," wrote author Earl Shorris, "helped along by the high level of education and the willingness to take on any challenge . . . and . . . a lack of reverence for persons or position. The Cuban exiles, primarily middle- and upper-middle-class, soon became middle- and upper-middle-class again."

In 1960, for example, Carlos Arboleya brought his family out of Cuba into Miami. According to authors Antón and Hernández, he left behind a lucrative job with the Banco Continental Cubano because all the banks had been taken over by the government. "I came with my wife, my one-year-old son and $40," he said. "We stayed in a room in a little old lady's home for $5 a week. Banks wouldn't hire me even though I had 16 years of experience in business." Arboleya took a job in a local factory, but it proved to be only a stepping stone to far better positions. By the middle of the decade, Arboleya had achieved the important position of president of Fidelity National Bank.

From his position at the bank, Arboleya loaned money to other Cuban immigrants who wanted to set up new businesses in South Florida. They established *bodegas*—small grocery stores—and restaurants in a Cuban section of Miami known as Little Havana and outside the city in Hialeah. At first, the Cuban immigrants hoped that their stay in the United States would be temporary. They expected that Castro would soon be overthrown and they could return to their homeland. But they were mistaken.

THE CUBAN MISSILE CRISIS AND AFTERWARD

In 1962, President John F. Kennedy learned that the Soviet Union was building long-range nuclear missile installations in Cuba. These might be used in an attack on the United States. Kennedy demanded that the Soviets remove the missile installations. In an agreement designed to avoid a nuclear war, Soviet leader Nikita Khrushchev destroyed the

BAY OF PIGS INVASION

In April 1961, approximately 1,500 Cuban exiles participated in an invasion of the island, organized by President John F. Kennedy, aimed at toppling the Castro government. The exiles, formed into Brigade 2506, had been trained in Guatemala, Panama and Nicaragua by the United States government. On April 15, 1961, three American planes with Cuban pilots bombed the air fields in Cuba, hoping to knock out Castro's small air force. But they were unsuccessful. Two days later, the small army of exiles approached the Bay of Pigs on the south coast of Cuba. Their landing ships were bombed by the Cuban air force, but the exiles still established a beachhead on the island. Nevertheless, they were soon overwhelmed by the Cuban army and forced to surrender. While some of the exiles were executed, most of them were imprisoned in Cuba. They were eventually returned to the United States for $53 million in food and medical supplies.

installations. In return, Kennedy promised not to launch any future invasions against Cuba.

Before the event, which was called the Cuban missile crisis, Castro had been encouraging immigrants to leave for the United States because it was easier than dealing with opposition to his regime. After the crisis ended, Castro cut off new immigration to the mainland. But Cubans continued to leave. They could still legally travel to other countries in South America, and from there they flew to North America.

Then in 1965, Castro decided to allow immigrants to travel directly to North America once again. For a short period, boats were permitted to travel to the Cuban port of Camarioca to pick up those who wanted to leave the island. But Castro refused to permit professionals, such as doctors, to emigrate because they were considered vital to Cuban society. The boatlift was followed by Freedom Flights, as they were called. The administration of President Lyndon B. Johnson reached an agreement with Castro, permitting more Cubans to leave via airplane to Miami. These Freedom Flights continued until 1973, bringing approximately 250,000 people off the island. These were primarily blue- collar workers, such as those who worked in factories and small-shop owners. The Cuban government had taken over their businesses, and these immigrants wanted to reestablish themselves in the United States.

In 1966, President Lyndon B. Johnson had also approved the Cuban Adjustment Act. The Cuban immigrants could now become permanent residents of the United States. Many Cubans decided to take advantage of the law because it meant that professionals, such as doctors and lawyers, could now qualify to practice in Florida.

In addition to the Cuban communities in Florida, other immigrants had moved northward to New Jersey, New York, Chicago, and even as far west as Los Angeles. Sometimes they were confronted with discrimination, seeing signs in some towns that said No Pets, No Children and No Cubans. But many immigrants overcame these conditions, finding acceptance from Anglos and even success.

Among these were Cuban immigrants who became successful major-league baseball players. Luis Tiant, for example, was a star pitcher with the Cleveland Indians and Boston Red Sox, while Pedro "Tony" Oliva won three batting titles with the Minnesota Twins. And in 2000, Atanasio (Tony) Pérez was voted into the Baseball Hall of Fame at Cooperstown, New York.

While many Cuban immigrants adjusted to life in the United States, some never gave up their efforts to bring about a change in the government that ruled their island. A few participated in guerrilla raids aimed at the Communist regime. They landed secretly on the island, blew up sugar mills, and hoped to stir up the population to revolt against the Castro government. Others joined the Federation of Cuban Students or a group called Abdala and led protest marches against the Communist dictatorship.

Cuban refugees, granted political asylum in The United States, arrive at Miami airport after coming off a plane from Cuba.

But these protests made no impact on the Castro regime.

By 1970, more than 400,000 Cuban immigrants lived in the United States, and most of them had settled into their new lives as residents of the mainland.

CASA BOU
1657 RADIOS TELEVISION RECORDS 1657
RADIO REPAIRS RECORDS
CARIBE
RCA VICTOR RECORDS
PIRAGUA
5¢

CHAPTER FOUR

The Puerto Rican Experience

THE ISLAND OF PUERTO RICO, A COLONY OF
Spain since the sixteenth century, had been conquered
by the United States during the Spanish-American War
in 1898. In the twentieth century, Puerto Rico had become an
American commonwealth. That is, the island had its own governor, and Puerto Ricans were citizens of the United States. But
they could not vote in presidential elections or elect representa-
tives to Congress. During the 1950s, Puerto Rican governor
Luis Muñoz Marín transformed the island from an agricultural
to an industrialized economy. Tens of thousands of Puerto
Ricans were forced to leave the poverty of the countryside for
the cities, but there were not enough jobs for everyone.
Therefore, the government encouraged immigration to the

Opposite:
Children in 1950s
Spanish Harlem
line up on a
sidewalk to buy
ices from a street
vendor.

United States. Puerto Ricans were told about job opportunities in North America and were given low-cost air fares to travel there.

Some Puerto Ricans came to North America to work in the tobacco fields outside of Hartford, Connecticut, and in other areas. Many others headed for New York City. They lived in Spanish Harlem, where a Puerto Rican community had been growing since the 1920s in an area known as El Barrio. There, Puerto Ricans could speak Spanish and gather together in hometown clubs at restaurants and bars.

With job opportunities plentiful in the United States, Puerto Ricans line up to board a plane in San Juan, that will take them to the United States.

These clubs included people who came from the same town in Puerto Rico and frequently knew one another. The clubs created a sense of community in a city that seemed hostile to Puerto Rican immigrants. Puerto Ricans often faced discrimination from Anglos. Since the conquest of Puerto Rico in the late nineteenth century, some North Americans looked down on Puerto Ricans. They considered them as inferior, uneducated people who were suited only for low-paying jobs.

Like Mexican immigrants, Puerto Ricans found work in unskilled jobs, frequently in the garment industry. They worked long hours sewing clothing at very low wages. Puerto Ricans were often prevented from finding better-paying jobs because they did not speak English. Some immigrants opened their own small businesses in the barrio. These included bodegas, which sold Hispanic foods. Immigrants also opened travel agencies and restaurants specializing in Puerto Rican cuisine. The travel agencies did a brisk business because many Puerto Ricans often returned to the island to visit their families. Others immigrated to the United States for just a short time before they decided to return home. On the island, they could speak Spanish and enjoy their own culture without experiencing discrimination.

Much of this discrimination was aimed at Puerto Rican children who attended the New York City schools. Because they did not speak English, it was difficult for them to learn.

In addition, most of the teachers were Anglos who did not speak Spanish and did very little to help the Puerto Rican children. Some believe this was one reason why approximately 80 percent of these children dropped out of school and failed to receive a high school diploma.

Responding to this problem, Hispanic leaders founded the Puerto Rican Forum in 1957 to focus on what to do about the high dropout rate. Hispanic leaders in the forum were also concerned about what was known as the "Puerto Rican Problem." Thousands of immigrants lived in run-down housing, scraping by on little money to buy food and clothing for themselves or their children. They faced a situation that was similar to Mexican immigrants working in the agricultural fields.

THE 1960s

The poverty experienced by many Puerto Rican families during the 1950s continued in the following decade. An estimated 70 percent of all Puerto Rican children born during the 1960s dropped out of high school without receiving their diplomas.

But by the mid-1960s, social change was occurring across the United States. In response to a civil rights movement led by African Americans, the Johnson administration spearheaded new legislation aimed at ending decades of inequality. Faced with many challenges and some hostility from the Anglo community, Puerto Ricans also began to form civil rights groups to improve their living and working conditions.

In 1964, Evelina López Antonetty, a Puerto Rican leader in New York, organized the United Bronx Parents organization. They joined with African Americans to protest discrimination in schools. Edna Acosta-Belén and Carlos Santiago, authors of *Puerto Ricans in the United States* wrote, "the licensing of Puerto Rican and Latino teachers in general was curtailed by the practices of the New York City Board of Education and powerful teacher unions . . . which were controlled by the white majority. It was com-

While children in many schools in the 1960s faced segregation, the children at the Benjamin Franklin School in Chicago, Illinois, did not have those problems. Caucasian, African, Puerto Rican, and Mexican children all study together at this school.

mon practice for a Puerto Rican teacher with a Spanish accent to be denied a license by the board and relegated to the corps of auxiliary teachers with limited possibilities for advancing their careers." Antonetty and her organization called for an end to this practice.

In 1968, Congress passed the Bilingual Education Act, led by Senator Joseph Montoya of New Mexico—the only Hispanic member of the U.S. Senate. Instead of forcing Spanish-speaking children into English classes when they entered, schools would now teach their courses in Spanish. As they learned English, the children would then be placed in classrooms with Anglo children. Bilingual education was aimed at giving Puerto Rican and other Hispanic children a better opportunity to succeed in school, reducing the high dropout rate.

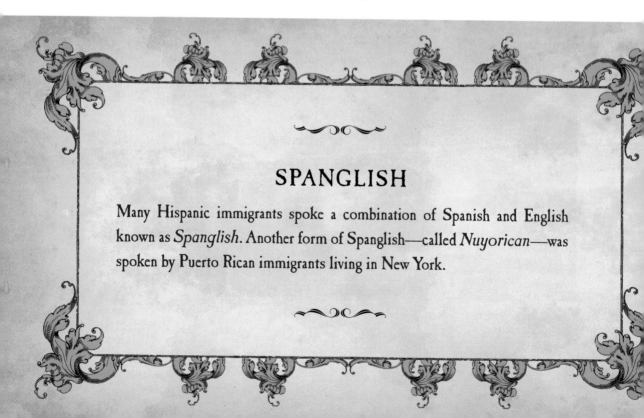

SPANGLISH

Many Hispanic immigrants spoke a combination of Spanish and English known as *Spanglish*. Another form of Spanglish—called *Nuyorican*—was spoken by Puerto Rican immigrants living in New York.

Meanwhile, a Puerto Rican youth organization known as ASPIRA had been founded in the early 1960s to encourage Hispanic children to become successful. ASPIRA, which means *aspire* in Spanish, was the brainchild of Antonia Pantoja, who had helped organize the Puerto Rican Forum. Born in San Juan in 1922, she attended the University of Puerto Rico and immigrated to the United States in 1944. Later, Pantoja graduated from Hunter College in New York and received a master's degree from Columbia University.

The primary goal of ASPIRA was building a positive sense of self among Puerto Rican young people. A mentoring program paired adults with young persons to encourage youth to stay in school, graduate, and attend college. "Yes, you can achieve your dream and go to college. Yes, you can do it" was the saying that guided the mentoring program. Another program developed by ASPIRA, called APEX, was aimed at getting parents involved in the education of their children so their children would complete their homework and perform well in school.

Another group, called the Puerto Rican Family Institute, was founded in 1960. The PRFI was aimed at helping families in New York obtain health care for their children, providing mental health services for families struggling in poverty, and promoting education.

Meanwhile, change was occurring among Puerto Rican immigrants in Chicago, where the Hispanic population had

HERMAN BADILLO

During the 1960s, only a few Puerto Rican immigrants achieved positions of political power. Among them was Herman Badillo, born in Caguas, Puerto Rico, in 1929. After he lost his parents to tuberculosis when he was only eleven, Badillo went to New York, where he was raised by his aunt. He graduated from City College of New York in 1951 and later obtained a law degree from Brooklyn Law School. After becoming a member of the Caribe Democratic Club in 1958, Badillo worked in the campaign of John F. Kennedy, who was elected president in 1960. Soon afterward he was selected by New York mayor Robert Wagner to work in his administration. In 1965, Badillo won election as Bronx borough president, running one of New York City's five boroughs—geographical areas—of Manhattan. He was the first Puerto Rican to hold this position. In 1970, Badillo won election to Congress, the first Puerto Rican to become a U.S. representative.

reached almost 250,000. Most Puerto Ricans held low-paying jobs and lived in a barrio around Clark Street, called "La Clark." In 1966, a young Puerto Rican named Arcelis Cruz was shot by a white policeman. The Puerto Rican community regarded this act as an example of police brutality, because Cruz had not been carrying a weapon. Riots broke out in Chicago on June 12 and continued for three days.

Following the riots, the Chicago Commission on Human Rights opened discussions among Puerto Rican residents to consider the discrimination that existed in the city. As a result of the riots and the discussions, Puerto Ricans formed a variety of organizations aimed at combating poor housing conditions, inadequate schools for Hispanic youth, and police brutality in Chicago. Among the groups that participated in these programs was the Young Lords.

Founded in 1959 by Orlando Davila, the Young Lords was originally a street gang that had been formed to deal with violence from white gangs against the Puerto Rican community. During the 1960s, the Lords were led by Jose "Cha-Cha" Jimenez, who gradually transformed them from a street gang into an agent of change. They set up a free breakfast program for children and planned to open a day care center.

Plans called for the center to be located in a local Methodist church. When white members of the church tried to stop the center from opening, the Young Lords took over the building. Soon afterward they faced an investigation from city health inspectors, who found violations

in the day care facility. Dealing with these violations cost ten thousand dollars. But with the help of contributions from supporters, the Young Lords paid for the violations and opened the center.

CULTURAL RENAISSANCE

During the 1950s and 1960s, Puerto Rican immigrants led a movement that shone a spotlight on their culture. In 1959, they organized the first Puerto Rican Day parade in New York City. Edna Acosta-Belén and Carlos Santiago wrote, "Town mayors back in Puerto Rico would bring delegations to New York City to participate in the parade," along with city residents, politicians, and well-known celebrities. Similar parades were also held in cities such as Chicago, Illinois and Hartford, Connecticut, which had large Puerto Rican communities. They featured salsa music—a mix

Opposite:
The Puerto Rican Day parade first took place in 1959. These young majorettes march up Fifth Avenue in New York City in 1975. The parade still takes place annually.

of Latin American rhythms—that was popularized by band-leaders such as Tito Puente.

Meanwhile, Puerto Rican writers were publishing works that described the experiences of immigrants trying to adjust to an Anglo culture in the United States. In the early 1950s, René Marqués had already published his play *La Carreta* (*The Oxcart*). Born in Arecibo, Puerto Rico, in 1919, Marqués wrote his play during the 1940s. It was staged in San Juan in 1951 and later opened in Manhattan in 1954. The play described a Puerto Rican family who had left the countryside trying to find a new life in San Juan and later in New York. Instead they found only poverty and had to deal with the death of their oldest son.

Pedro Juan Soto, another writer, was born in Cataño, Puerto Rico, in 1928. He later moved to New York City, where he received a college degree from Long Island University. He is best known for a collection of stories called *Spiks*, an alternative spelling for a negative term used by Anglos to describe Hispanic immigrants. His stories described the struggles of immigrants trying to succeed on the mainland.

Piri Thomas, another writer, was born in Spanish Harlem in 1928. As he grew up, Thomas became a member of a gang, committing violent crimes that eventually sent him to prison. After his release, Thomas published his autobiography, *Down These Mean Streets,* in 1967. One of the issues that Thomas explored was the racism he encountered in the United States. Since he had a dark skin, Anglos believed that Thomas was an African American, and he became the object of racism. Within the Hispanic community, there was also a form of racism. Those with dark skins were regarded as inferior to light-skinned Hispanic immigrants, who considered themselves white. In addition to *Down These Mean Streets*, Thomas also published *Stories from El Barrio*.

The writings of Thomas and other authors helped raise awareness of the Puerto Rican experience across the United States.

CHAPTER FIVE

VIVA CHICANO!

IN 1967, RODOLFO "CORKY" GONZALES WROTE about the same feelings of inferiority among Mexican Americans that had led Puerto Rican writers to speak out. His poem "I am Joaquín" spoke for millions of Hispanic people:

> I am Joaquín,
> lost in a world of confusion,
> caught up in the whirl of a
> gringo society,
> confused by the rules,
> scorned by attitudes,
> suppressed by manipulation,
> and destroyed by modern society.

Gonzales's poem was widely circulated in Mexican American communities across the United States and helped

Opposite: Rodolfo "Corky" Gonzales speaks during a Chicano conference.

spark the Chicano movement. This movement was also inspired by César Chávez and the NFWA. In the past, the word *Chicano* had been a negative term used by Anglos— gringos—to describe Mexican Americans. But during the late 1960s, it came to symbolize the pride that Mexican Americans, born in the United States, began to take in their history, their culture, and their language.

Rodolfo Gonzales was born in Denver, Colorado, in 1928 and grew up in the city's Eastside Barrio. An emotional youth who was regularly "popping off like a cork," according to an uncle, friends and family gave him the nickname Corky. Gonzales attended high school and worked in the beet fields around Colorado. He hoped to attend college, but he did not have enough money to earn a degree from the University of Denver. During the early 1950s, he earned a national reputation as an excellent amateur boxer.

Later, he became a business owner in Denver, Colorado, and was involved in the Viva Kennedy movement during the 1960 presidential election. In the 1960s, he became a local leader of the War on Poverty program, initiated by President Lyndon B. Johnson. But Johnson's commitment to domestic poverty programs declined as he broadened America's involvement in the Vietnam War. Gonzales was highly critical of the war, which claimed the lives of an increasing number of minority soldiers.

In 1968, Gonzales served as one of the leaders of the Poor People's Campaign in Washington, D.C. Thousands

HISPANIC AMERICANS AND
THE VIETNAM WAR

Many white young men avoided being drafted by the U.S. government because they were in college. Since only a small number of African American and Hispanic youth entered college, a higher percentage of them were drafted into the military and sent to Vietnam. According to Ruben Treviso, author of *Vietnam Reconsidered*, one half of all Hispanics who went to Vietnam were in combat. And about 20 percent of the Hispanic soldiers died there. The casualty rate among Hispanics was more than 50 percent higher than among Anglo soldiers. The high number of casualties deeply saddened the Hispanic American community, but it also inspired them to organize to protest the war and to increase their political power in the United States. They wanted to prevent the same situation from occurring again in the future.

of protesters from across the United States went to Washington, D.C., to demand a greater commitment by the Johnson administration to solve the problems of the poor. Shortly afterward, Gonzales brought together a large group of Chicano youth in Denver at a meeting held in March 1969. It was called the Crusade for Justice. Young Mexican

Americans discussed a variety of issues, including the war in Vietnam, inequality in public schools, and discrimination in housing and employment. This was the first national conference of Chicano youth.

The conference also addressed the concept of *Aztlán*. This refers to the origins of Chicano culture in Mexico among the powerful Aztec Indians, who ruled the region during the fifteenth century. The Aztecs created a thriving civilization that was eventually conquered by the Spanish in the early sixteenth century. Aztlán became a way of emphasizing the rich heritage of Mexican Americans, an important method of asserting their pride, and an integral part of the Chicano movement.

REIES LÓPEZ TIJERINA

Another Chicano leader who participated in the Poor People's Campaign was Reies López Tijerina. He was known as *El Tigre*, the Tiger. Born in Laredo, Texas, in 1926, Tijerina was a dynamic preacher who established a community for his followers in southern Arizona. In 1959, he led a strike among cotton workers and forced a local farm owner to increase their wages. During the early 1960s, Tijerina formed *La Alianza Federal de Mercedes*, the Federal Alliance of Land Grants. The goal of La Alianza was to recover all the land owned by Mexican farmers before the Treaty of Guadalupe Hidalgo ended the Mexican War in 1848. Under the terms of the treaty, the land owned by

In 1972, Reies
López Tijerina
speaks about
Chicano rights in
New Mexico.

Mexican farmers in Texas, New Mexico, and Arizona was supposed to be protected by law. However, during the following decades, it was illegally claimed by Anglo land owners who gradually took control of it.

Under Tijerina's leadership, La Alianza published a newspaper publicizing the claims of Mexican Americans to the land and broadcast a daily radio program, known as "The Voice of Justice." In 1966, Tijerina and some of his supporters took over a piece of land in the Kit Carson National Forest in New Mexico, which they claimed was part of a land grant owned by Mexican Americans. Two forest rangers were arrested by La Alianza but later set free. As author Stan Steiner explained, Tijerina wrote that "For as long as the ownership of property is the basic foundation of our society, everyone has a vested interest in the protection of property . . . so that thieves will not inherit the earth."

In 1966 and again in 1967, Tijerina led marches to Austin, the Texas capital, hoping to convince the governor to recognize the old Mexican land claims. But nothing happened. Later in 1967, La Alianza planned to hold a meeting in the small village of Coyote, New Mexico. When the local district attorney, Alfonso Sánchez, tried to prevent the meeting, Tijerina led his followers to the courthouse. There he planned to arrest Sánchez. Instead, a gun battle broke out, and two policemen were hit by the gunfire. Tijerina fled with the other members of La Alianza, but they were later arrested.

The arrest became front-page news. Tijerina received the support of Corky Gonzales, who brought a large group of people to the jail where El Tigre was being held. Tried for kidnapping and assault, Tijerina was found not guilty. But he was later convicted for his activities at Kit

In 2007, Reies López Tijerina invited friends and family to his home in Coyote, New Mexico, to celebrate the fortieth anniversary of the day he led twenty activists in a raid on the courthouse.

Carson National Forest and sent to prison. Without his leadership, La Alianza fell apart.

THE STRENGTH OF THE CHICANO MOVEMENT

While these events were occurring in the Southwest, the Chicano movement continued to grow. Among its foremost leaders were César Chávez and Dolores Huerta, cofounders of the United Farm Workers of America. During the late 1960s, the union continued using strikes, boycotts, and tough bargaining to win new contracts with the large growers in California.

Elsewhere in California, students in East Los Angeles staged a walkout in March 1968 to protest discrimination in their high schools. This was the same period of massive student demonstrations against the war in Vietnam. The East Los Angeles walkouts were led by a Chicano teacher, Sal Castro, who was a member of the faculty at Lincoln High School. As the protests spread to other schools, police were called in to break up the walkout. Castro and twelve students were arrested, but Castro was later released. According to author Earl Shorris, "It was the first time Mexican Americans in East Los Angeles had made a powerful expression of their discontent." Although the demonstration had focused attention on the problems in high schools, few changes occurred to improve conditions there.

Two years after the Los Angeles walkouts, a demonstration occurred in San Diego, California. The Logan Heights

BROWN BERETS

Among the leaders of the demonstrations in Los Angeles was a group calling themselves the Brown Berets. In 1966, high school students had met at the Annual Chicano Student Conference in Los Angeles to talk about conditions in the barrios. Some of these students later formed the Young Citizens for Community Action. In 1967, they began wearing brown berets to protest discrimination in  public schools, police brutality, and poor housing in the barrios. "The brown beret was chosen," the group said, "because it is a symbol of the love and pride we have in our race and in the color of our skin." The Brown Berets were dedicated to protecting young people in the barrio from the police. Along with Sal Castro, the Brown Berets organized the East Los Angeles demonstrations in 1968. The following year, several members of the organization began publishing a newspaper, *La Causa* (The Chicano Cause). In addition, they organized breakfast programs for children and medical clinics to serve the poor, free of charge. Brown Berets also joined the Poor People's Campaign in Washington as well as the Crusade for Justice in Denver, Colorado.

area, known as Barrio Logan, was home to a large Hispanic community. During the 1960s, the government built a large interstate highway through part of the barrio. It destroyed thousands of homes and businesses, changing the entire face of the community. The residents wanted the city council to build a park in the barrio in return for damaging their neighborhoods. Instead of a park, however, the city decided to build a parking lot. Led by a Brown Beret named Mario Solis, students streamed out of their high schools and staged a sit-in at the proposed parking lot. The protest continued for twelve days. City officials talked with local residents during the sit-in, and they finally agreed to build Chicano Park. Construction began immediately. During the early 1970s, Chicano artists created a large number of outdoor murals and sculptures to beautify the park.

Chicano Park and its murals became a tribute to the strength of the Chicano movement. It also symbolized the growing importance and power of Hispanic Americans during the decades of the 1950s and 1960s. They had entered politics, formed powerful unions, achieved enormous economic gains, and launched a dynamic cultural movement. As a result, they were playing an increasingly significant role in American society.

TIMELINE

1948	G.I. Forum founded
	Ed Roybal elected to Los Angeles City Council
1952	César Chávez joins Community Service Organization
1957	Puerto Rican Forum begun
1959	Fidel Castro comes to power in Cuba
	Young Lords started
1961	Bay of Pigs invasion launched
	Puerto Rican Family Institute founded
	Mexican-American Political Association founded
1962	Cuban missile crisis occurs
	Roybal elected to Congress, first Mexican American since nineteenth century
	Chávez and Dolores Huerta begin Farm Workers Association
1963	President John F. Kennedy assassinated
1964	United Bronx Parents organization launched
1965	Great Delano Grape Strike begins
1966	Farm Workers Association wins contract with Schenley Company
	Cuban Adjustment Act passed
1967	Rudolfo Gonzales publishes "I am Joaquín"
	Brown Berets formed
	Piri Thomas publishes *Down These Mean Streets*
1968	Congress passes Bilingual Education Act
	Rev. Dr. Martin Luther King Jr. assassinated
	Poor People's Campaign occurs in Washington D.C.
	East Los Angeles walkouts occur
1969	Crusade for Justice held in Denver, Colorado
1970	Herman Badillo becomes first Puerto Rican congressman
	Chicano Park begun

GLOSSARY

aztlán A term that refers to the origins of Mexican culture.

barrio Hispanic neighborhood.

bodega Small Hispanic market.

Bracero program Effort to bring Mexican workers into the United States.

Chicano Mexican American born in the United States.

coyotes People who bring illegal immigrants into the United States.

El Norte North America.

guerrillas Members of a small unit making surprise attacks on a regular army.

Hispanic Americans Americans from Spanish speaking countries.

huelga Strike.

La Alianza Federal de Mercedes Organization dedicated to regaining Mexican American lands.

mutualistas Hispanic self-help organizations.

visa Permission for a visitor from a foreign country to enter the United States

wetbacks An offensive term used to describe a Mexican, especially a laborer, who crosses the U.S. border illegally.

FURTHER INFORMATION

BOOKS

Conley, Kate. *The Puerto Rican Americans*. San Diego: Lucent Books, 2005.

Taus-Bolstad, Stacy. *Puerto Ricans in America*. Minneapolis: Lerner Publications, 2005.

Worth, Richard. *Dolores Huerta*. New York: Chelsea House, 2006.

WEB SITES

ASPIRA Association
www.aspira.org
> The only national nonprofit organization devoted solely to the education and leadership development of Puerto Rican and other Latino youth

The Chicago Public Library
www.chipublib.org/004chicago/disasters/riots_19666to1977.html
> Information about the 1966–1977 riots in Chicago, Illinois

The Library of Congress
www.loc.gov/rr/hispanic
> Hispanic Americans in Congress

LULAC—League of United Latin American Citizens
http://www.lulac.org/about/history.html
> Working to bring about positive social and economic changes for Hispanic Americans

BIBLIOGRAPHY

Acosta-Belén, Edna, and Carlos E. Santiago. *Puerto Ricans in the United States: A Contemporary Portrait*. Boulder, CO: Lynne Rienner, 2006.

Antón, Alex, and Roger E. Hernández. *Cubans in America*. New York: Kensington Books, 2002.

Del Castillo, Richard Griswold, and Richard A. Garcia. *César Chávez: A Triumph of the Spirit*. Norman, OK: University of Oklahoma Press, 1996.

Gutiérrez, David, ed. *The Columbia History of Latinos in the United States Since 1960*. New York: Columbia University Press, 2004.

Padilla, Felix M., ed. *Handbook of Hispanic Cultures in the United States: Sociology, Vol 3*. Houston: Arte Público Press, 1994.

Stavans, Ilan. *Latino History and Culture: The Ultimate Question and Answer Book*. New York: HarperCollins, 2007.

INDEX

Hartford (CT), Puerto Rican Americans in, 50, 59
Hispanic people. See Cuban Americans; Filipino Americans; Mexican Americans; Puerto Rican Americans
huelgas. *See* strikes
Huerta, Dolores, 32, 70

"I am Joaquin" (poem, Gonzales), 63–64
immigrants, illegal, 9, 14, 18–21, **19**, **20**, 32
 see also Cuban Americans; Filipino Americans; Mexican Americans; Puerto Rican Americans

Jimenez, Jose "Cha-Cha," 57
jobs, discrimination in, 8–10, 16–21, 27, 29, 32–35, 50–51, 57
Johnson, Lyndon B., 45, 52, 64

Kennedy, John F., 29, 43, 44, 45, 64
Khrushchev, Nikita, 43, 45

La Alianza Federal de Mercedes, 66–68, 70
land, protests over, 67–68
League of United Latin American Citizens (LULAC), 11–12
Little Schools of the 400, 12
Los Angeles (CA), Mexican Americans in, 5, 6, 11, 13–14, 26, 70–72

marches, **33**, 34, 35, 46–47, 68
Marqués, René, 60
Mendez v. Westminster School District, 11
Mexican American Political Association (MAPA), 29, 30
Mexican Americans, 5–35, 42, 63–72
Mexican War (1846–1848), 6, 7, 66
Mexico, revolution in, 8–9
Miami (FL), Cuban Americans in, 37, 40, 42–43, **47**
migrant worker movement, 23, 24, 25, 29, **31**, 31–35
Montoya, Joseph, 54
Muñoz, Luis Marin, 49
mutualistas, 31

National Farm Workers Association (NFWA), 31–35, **33**, 64
National Farm Workers Union, 34–35
National Mexican Brotherhood, 30
New York City, Puerto Rican Americans in, **48**, 50–51, 54, **58**, 59
Nuyorican, 54

Oliva, Pedro "Tony," 46
Operation Peter Pan, 40–42
Operation Wetback, 20–21

Pantoja, Antonia, 55
Pérez, Atanasio (Tony), 46
police brutality, 13, 26, 57, 71
Poor People's Campaign, 64–65, 66, 71
poverty, 28, 49, 52
Puerto Rican Americans, 42, **48**, 49–61, **50**
Puerto Rican Day parade, **58**, 59–60
Puerto Rican Family Institute (PRFI), 55
Puerto Rican Forum, 52, 55

racism, 60–61
 see also civil rights movement; discrimination
railroad work, 8
ranch work, 8
refugees, Cuban American, 40–42, 45, **47**
Rio Grande River, crossing, 18, **19**
Ross, Fred, 14, **15**, 16, 25–26
Roybal, Edward R., 5–6, **13**, 13–16, **15**, 20, 26, 29

salsa music, 59–60
Schenley Corporation, 34–35
schools, **41**, **53**
 discrimination in, 9–12, 24–25, 51–55
 protests in, 71, 72
Soto, Pedro Juan, 60
Soviet Union, 18–19, 38–39, 43
Spain, settlers from, **4**, 5
Spanglish, 54
Spanish (language), 11, 24, 51, 52, 54
Spanish Harlem (New York City), **48**, 50
strikes, 32–35, 70

Subversive Registration Bill, 19–20

teachers, Hispanic, 53–54
   see also schools
Texas, Mexican Americans in, 9–12, 28, 29
Thomas, Piri, 60–61
Tiant, Luis, 46
Tijerina, Reies López, 66–70, **67**, **69**
travel agencies, Puerto Rican, 51
Treaty of Guadalupe Hidalgo, 6, 66

unions, 30–35, 64, 70
United Bronx Parents, 53
United Farm Workers of America, 70
United States, war with Mexico, 6, 7, 66

Vietnam War, 64, 65, 70
Viva Kennedy Clubs, 29, 64
voter registration, 13–14, 26–27, **27**, 29

wetbacks, 18, 20–21
white people. See Anglos, discrimination
by
World War II, 12, 14, 17
writers, Puerto Rican, 60

Young Citizens for Community Award, 71
Young Lords, 57, 59

ABOUT THE AUTHOR

RICHARD WORTH is the author of more than fifty books, including biographies, historical works, and current events. He has written two books for Marshall Cavendish, *The Arab-Israeli Conflict* and *Workers' Rights*. He is also the author of a biography of Dolores Huerta, the cofounder of the United Farm Workers of America, and a history of Mexican immigration.